Anne Horsfall has lived in Dorset for many years and is a botanist with a first-hand understanding of wild flowers and woodland in the county. She has researched plant habitat change in Dorset, and has contributed articles to the *Proceedings of the Dorset Natural History and Archaeological Society.* She wrote the coastal and woodland chapters of *The Natural History of Dorset,* and much of the woodland chapter has been incorporated into the second part of the present book.

Following page
The nocturnal wood mouse, or long-tailed field mouse,
is common throughout woodlands in Dorset,
building its burrow amongst decomposing vegetation in
complex underground tunnel systems.

DISCOVER DORSET

WOODLANDS

ANNE HORSFALL

THE DOVECOTE PRESS

Britain's largest ladybird, the eyed ladybird, lives in
Dorset's conifer plantations.

First published in 2003 by The Dovecote Press Ltd
Stanbridge, Wimborne, Dorset BH21 4JD

ISBN 1 904349 11 0

© Anne Horsfall 2003

Anne Horsfall has asserted her rights under the Copyright, Designs
and Patent Act 1988 to be identified as author of this work

Series designed by Humphrey Stone

Typeset in Monotype Sabon
Printed and bound in Singapore

A CIP catalogue record for this book is available
from the British Library

CONTENTS

INTRODUCTION

What impressions might a traveller moving westward across Dorset gain of the county's woodland? First the lack of any historic forest as extensive as the New Forest he has just left behind. Soon, however, his attention might be drawn to the large conifer plantations clothing much of the former heathland across east and south Dorset. If his cross-county route lay further north over the chalklands he will see the coppiced woodlands of Cranborne Chase and the sloping beechwoods around Bulbarrow and Milton Abbas. Continuing on through north and west Dorset, he will look down on the broad pastoral landscapes of the Blackmore and Marshwood Vales, a countryside of smaller oakwoods – of copses, thickets, hedges and irregular fields dotted with trees – much like the landscape of Thomas Hardy's *The Woodlanders*. Should he have read the novel our imaginary traveller might recall how hard was the work needed to maintain such an apparently idyllic scene, and how woodlands lay at the heart of the local economy.

Dorset, in common with the rest of lowland England, was almost entirely covered with natural broadleaved woodland after the last Ice Age. As the ice retreated northwards, 12-15,000 years ago, the tundra which followed in its wake became colonised by pioneer scrub followed by a more stable mixed woodland, with oak, ash, elm, lime and many other trees and shrubs. This blanketing natural woodland, which had to be cleared if the land it covered was to be used, has become known as the 'wild-wood'.

As the population increased, more of the wild-wood was felled, initially mainly to clear land for agriculture. The woodland to survive the longest was usually on the heavier clays and soils too damp for cultivation. In Dorset, as throughout lowland Britain, woods on every type of soil have been continuously cut, coppiced and replanted to provide for a succession of changing needs.

Landscape historians and conservationists have tried to define the various types of woodland found in Britain today. The few woods that have a direct link with the wild-wood are called primary woodlands. Woodland on land that was cleared but then re-wooded and which has borne trees continuously since at least 1600 is known as ancient. Woods that have clearly re-colonised bare ground, or been planted, are called secondary woods. In Dorset, as elsewhere, it is the scattered remnants of ancient woodland that are the most significant.

To ecologists, the age and origins of a wood are of great importance, not simply for historical reasons, but also because the oldest woods tend to be richest in plant and animal species. Their complex soils, ancient coppice stools, and huge number of organisms, many of which we know little about, make them almost impossible to recreate. As we shall see later, there are plants that are exclusively confined to ancient woods.

Virtually all woods, whether ancient or not, have been influenced by man. In some, felling, cutting and coppicing have taken place for centuries. They may have lost some of the species of the original woodland, through a gradual process of selection, whilst at the same time acquiring others which have found the environment of a managed woodland to be congenial. Indeed many of the species which grow in Dorset's woods are adapted to traditional management regimes such as coppicing.

Today, less than 10% of Dorset lies under woodland, including plantations and other secondary woods: of this, only 2-3% can be described as ancient. Important remaining blocks of old woodland include Duncliffe, Piddles, Oakers, Chetterwood, Creech Great Wood, and those at Powerstock, Melbury, Edmonsham, Cranborne and on Cranborne Chase. There are many smaller, more isolated woods whose names also suggest ancient origins – such as Holt, Buckshaw, Aldermore, Tincleton Hanging, Birches Copse and Heron Coppice. Most Dorset estates also have boundary woods and plantings, usually of more recent origin, whose names – Botany Wood, Jubilee Plantation, Zariba Clump – often celebrate or commemorate some historical event.

The old Royal Forests, in contrast, were medieval institutions and royal hunting grounds, subject to forest laws. As well as woods and wood pasture, where grazing animals were admitted, the forests included open areas of heath, downland scrub, rough pastures and small settlements. Very little original woodland remains in the former Royal Forests of Dorset, but those pockets that do are of considerable interest. A brief history of each of Dorset's Royal Forests can be found beginning on page 27.

In addition to Dorset's broadleaved woodlands, there are widespread conifer plantations, ranging from small stands to extensive forests of non-native trees species, many of them established by the Forestry Commission over the last eighty years. These modern forest plantations are managed by Forest Enterprise to produce softwood timber, often for pulping, at Puddletown, Wareham, Moors Valley, Ferndown and elsewhere.

Today however, forestry is more in tune with public demand for wildlife and landscape conservation, so that these working forests are becoming more sustainable, varied and attractive to visit. Forest Enterprise is gradually diversifying its huge plantations in Dorset, encouraging both wildlife and people, and even returning some areas to heath. They will play an increasingly important role in conserving species that depend upon coniferous woodland; especially the birds of prey who require large territories and secure refuges. Forestry and conservation, so often in conflict during the twentieth century, may well find common cause during the twenty-first. The interaction of the vast array of plants and animals give woodland ecology a special fascination for anyone with an eye and ear for nature.

Opposite page: Judge Wyndham's Oak, Silton.
This ancient oak marks the centre of a medieval village that was probably abandoned nearly four hundred years ago.

PART I

Ancient Woodland

WOODLAND HISTORY IN DORSET

When the Saxons settled in Dorset in the sixth century much of the primary wild-wood had already disappeared. Several thousand years of continuous settlement by Neolithic, Bronze Age, Iron Age, Roman and Romano-British people had significantly cleared the extensive broadleaved forests that once covered much of the county. The Saxons continued the transformation begun by their predecessors, creating a countryside still recognizable in many parts of Dorset today. Our hedges, villages, churches, parishes, and place-names are often Saxon in origin.

Because trees made obvious landmarks, Saxon charters describing parish boundaries are our first written mention of Dorset's trees. One of AD 894 defining the boundaries of Almer, near Sturminster

The crab apple, usually found isolated on the edge of woodland,
was frequently mentioned as a landmark in Saxon charters
defining parish boundaries.

A rare coppice of small-leaved lime in Boulsbury Wood, near Cranborne.

Marshall, in part reads: ' . . . from the Dagger thorn tree to a thorn thicket over against the Winterborne . . . along the Coombe to the wood . . . to the bank where the Sallow trees grow.' Remarkably, another slightly later charter of 935 mentions a wood, 'littlen wde', which survives to this day as the Little Wood at Chettle, and whose low sprawling bank on the southern side may be part of the original boundary.

The trees and shrubs named in the charters are familiar. Thorn is the commonest, followed by oak, ash, maple and apple, the latter including 'sour apple', or crab apple, and 'hore apple', which means a tree on a boundary. Willow is distinguished as withies or sallow. Alder and holly make infrequent appearances, but birch, hazel, broom, furse and elder are rarely mentioned. There is a single reference to a pear tree, now extinct as a wild tree, and a lime tree near Woodlands, where the rare small-leaved lime still flourishes. The absence of a tree as conspicuous as beech seems to confirm the view that it was not native to Dorset, but introduced later.

The Domesday Book of 1086 marks the first attempt to record the extent of Dorset's woods. Compared to the midland shires, Dorset was not well-wooded. Although the inclusion of woodland points to its importance as part of an estate, calculations based on Domesday show that approximately 13% of the county was woodland, much of it small and fragmented.

None of Dorset's Domesday woodland was recorded on the degraded soils of the heath, land which would have to wait until the arrival of the conifer in the nineteenth century before it could be planted. Of special interest is a total lack of woodland in the fertile coastal lands south of Dorchester and the Ridgeway, from Abbotsbury east to Lulworth, which had long been cleared for growing wheat and barley.

Domesday distinguishes the different kinds of woodland, usually either *silva* (woodland with timber trees) or *silva minuta* (underwood, including hazel). *Silva modica* is listed at Stoke Abbott and Stalbridge Weston, perhaps as larger underwood such as coppiced oak and ash. Renscombe, on the Purbeck coast, includes *silva infructosa*, or 'unproductive trees', meaning that acorns for pigs to feed on are absent – hardly surprising in a coastal coombe more suited to ash than oak.

The Domesday Book is a far from accurate guide to Dorset's largest woods in 1086. Many stood inside the Royal Forests or royal manors, which were made up of several often widely scattered settlements, and for which only a single total is given. For example, the royal manor of Wimborne Minster contained over eleven square miles of woodland, but much of it was fragmented, and the manor itself was enormous, embracing Holt, Wimborne St Giles, Shapwick, Pamphill, and today's Kingston Lacy. Of more help are the large areas of woodland listed in Ashmore, Cranborne and Hinton Martell, which all retain important woods today.

The pressure on Dorset's medieval woods undoubtedly increased as the population and demand for timber and farmland grew. The Black Death of 1349 and the successive outbreaks of plague that followed brought a temporary respite. Some villages were

Oak timbers from Dorset's medieval woods can still be seen in the hammer-beam roof and panelled screens in the Abbot's Hall, Milton Abbey, which was built in 1498.

abandoned, neglected land reverted to scrub and woodland. As prosperity returned, Dorset's downs became home to vast flocks of sheep. A balance had to be struck between the need for coppiced hazel for hurdles for folding the sheep and the appetite for more grazing land. Some of the wealth made by Dorset's wool merchants and landowners built its earliest surviving manor houses and extensions to its abbeys, as at Milton and Forde, where the great oak timbers can still be seen. But the price was high, particularly on the central chalk downland, which one Tudor traveller described as 'little corn, no wood, but all about great flokkes of sheppe.'

The Dissolution of the Monasteries in 1536 brought the biggest change of land ownership since the Norman Conquest. The estates belonging to Dorset's monastic houses covered more than a third of the county, all of which were acquired by Henry VIII and then sold off to a new landowning gentry. A little more than a century later the Civil War brought further changes. Royalist estates were confiscated, the land rented out, and any woodland was retained by Parliament for profit – as at Tarrant Keyneston Farm in 1646 where it was ordered 'that the woods bee put to sale, cut and disposed of . . . for the use of the State'.

Only occasionally did a measure of justice overcome parliamentary zeal, as in this entry concerning Lytchett Matravers from the Minute Book of the Standing Committe that administered Dorset on behalf of Parliament: 'James Gerrard . . . in regard of his great losses in the burninge of his house and all his goods within it . . . it was ordered that George Felleter should make sale of certain underwoods in a wood called Hell wood . . . for the benefit of the said Mr Gerrard'. Several woods called Hill Wood are still to be found near Lytchett Matravers.

More typical was the plea by the eighty-year-old John Tregonwell, who lived at Winterborne Anderson, and whose house and stock had been taken from him, that his woods should be spared and no timber felled.

Before the second half of the eighteenth century woods were rarely deliberately planted, but depended on natural regeneration for their regrowth. The best portrait of the state of Dorset's woods prior to the beginnings of widespread tree-planting is provided by Isaac Taylor's 1765 map of the county. The scale was an inch to the mile, large enough to include 200 woods, some of which were named. A few have disappeared, notably Hartgrove near West Orchard and Beaulieu Wood near Buckland Newton, and most are considerably smaller, reduced by the relentless demand of agriculture, but all those to survive can be regarded as ancient woodland. Apart from a scattering in the west, the greatest concentration of woodland follows the sweep of the tertiary clay soils from the south of the Blackmore Vale up to Cranborne Chase, and again from east of Dorchester to Wimborne and Cranborne. A smaller band extends from East Lulworth eastwards on both sides of the Purbeck Hills.

Dorset was undoubtedly poorly wooded in 1765. Oak, larch and

A fine oak tree in Melbury Park. Melbury's remarkable oaks are survivors of ancient woodland that was largely cleared following its enclosure as a Tudor deer park.

spruce were all being imported, and Dorset's towns were dependent on coal for fuel. A report to the Board of Agriculture published nearly thirty years later, in 1793, describes the county as 'extremely barren both in timber and wood'. The writer, John Claridge, mentions the fine oak timber at Melbury, Sherborne, and in parts of the Blackmore Vale. He also praises the new plantations on the Bryanston, Moreton and Milton Abbas estates. But his final verdict was that 'there was no part of England which he had ever seen so much in want of ornamental and useful woodland as Dorset.'

Both Isaac Taylor's map and John Claridge's report coincide with a period of profound change in the county. Enclosure turned the medieval open fields into neat rectangles bounded by thorn hedges. The expansion of trade and industry generated new wealth to the country estates, leading to the creation of spinneys and coverts for the

A detail from Isaac Taylor's 1765 map of Dorset.
The map marks the watershed between a reliance on existing ancient woodland to meet the demand for timber and the beginnings of more widespread planting. To the west of Bere Regis is Piddle Wood, still wooded today, whilst north-east of Moreton is Clouds Plantation, one of the earliest of the extensive late eighteenth century plantings by James Frampton. As well as including part of the army ranges, much of the open heathland shown on the map is now thick conifer with only occasional fragments of heath or older broadleaved trees.

fox and the pheasant, and the beginnings of more widespread planting. 'Capability' Brown's influence inspired many landowners to form parkland complete with clumps, plantations, and avenues. This new fashion for a 'natural' landscape, complete with serpentine lake, showed scant regard for any ancient woodland that did not fit into the overall scheme. Those at Holnest and Lulworth were destroyed.

Boundaries were straightened, banks grubbed out, new rides laid out. The Moreton Estate diary of 1758 records that 'a thousand trees of different sorts were planted in Snelling Grove and several hundred Scotch Firs in the centre and west part of Sares Wood'. Their descendants may still be seen today, in Sares Wood near Affpuddle and along Snelling Drove near Moreton. This was only the beginning. Between 1779-1781 James Frampton of Moreton planted 130,000 trees of 11 different types, a number which rose to 220,205 in 1783 alone.

The eighteenth century landscapes created by landowners like James Frampton are still familiar today. To them we owe many of Dorset's beech trees, planted extensively in avenues and along park and estate boundaries. Sycamore became widespread, notably in coastal areas, and alien shrubs such as laurel, box and rhododendron were planted to provide cover for pheasants. The tradition of tree-planting and well-managed forestry established on many Dorset estates at that time has endured into the present.

Planting of broadleaved trees and conifers continued throughout the Victorian period. The advent of the railways made cheap coal and coke widely available, causing the traditional management of coppices to embark on its long decline. Unprofitable coppices were grubbed out to meet the demand for agricultural land.

Dorset's woods were heavily exploited during both World Wars. The great eighteenth century parkland plantings, derided by one early commentator as 'preserved for ornament, and therefore of little use to the public', produced valuable quantities of timber. After 1919, and again after 1945, conifers were generally planted to replace woodland clear-felled in wartime. Dorset's ancient woodlands paid a particularly high price. Many were replanted with conifer, or conifer with beech, irrevocably changing their rich diversity to dark, impoverished habitats typical of pine, hemlock and spruce.

The last twenty years have seen a significant change in attitude, with a much greater emphasis on conservation. Woodland reserves are common throughout the county and ancient woods on private estates are now widely managed on traditional lines, with regular coppicing or replanting with oak and other broadleaved trees.

TRACING ANCIENT WOODLAND

Dorset's ancient woods and coppices are places of spreading oak trees and clumps of hazel, with ash, holly and other native trees and shrubs. They are rich wildlife habitats, and generally can be recognised by characteristics that set them apart from more modern plantings. Because they are on land that has continuously borne trees for at least 400 years, and the pressures on them throughout that time will have been considerable, they are usually small and isolated. Often ancient woods adjoin a parish boundary, beyond its meadows and arable fields, which in early settlements tended to be close to the village centre. Original wood boundaries are rarely straight, and their protective wood-banks are conspicuous, usually with a ditch on the outside. Any internal boundary banks are also irregular. They are sited on land that was usually unsuitable for farmland, often on steep north-facing slopes or heavy, poorly-drained clay soil. Yet these woodland soils are largely undisturbed and the top layers have a large and diverse population of invertebrates and many species of fungi, mosses and liverworts.

One important feature is often the large number of different types of trees and shrubs on the boundary of the wood, the one place usually unaffected by management activities in the wood itself. An example is the western edge of Clifton Wood (Clist Wood) on the undulating edge of the Clifton Maybank parish boundary (near Yeovil). Here are oak, ash, hazel, maple, aspen, grey willow, goat willow, hawthorn, blackthorn, elder, dogwood, spindle, privet and wayfaring-tree, whilst the wood itself contains small-leaved lime and wild service-tree, both of them rare. Further proof of Clifton Wood's longevity comes from a court case of 1292 concerning illegal felling, in which pear and apple are mentioned as well as oak and aspen.

An ancient wood may also be identified by dense expanses of bluebells and other spring flowers. Other wild flowers associated only

Bluebells under oak on the ramparts of the Iron Age hillfort at Coney's Castle, on the western rim of the Marshwood Vale. Dense drifts of bluebells can help identify ancient woodland.

with ancient woods include wood anemone, woodruff, wood vetch, wood spurge, toothwort, herb-paris, archangel, narrow-leaved lungwort, and several grasses and sedges. Bluebells have also survived for centuries in the open under bracken or on damp waysides where once there was woodland.

Another way of tracing ancient woodland is through place-names. Some village and farm names have a definite link with woodland or its clearance. Significantly, most such names are concentrated in the north and west of the county. Typical examples would be *bere, clinger, shaw, holt, frith* and *wood* – all of which are Anglo-Saxon wood-words, and were often combined with a personal name to describe a settlement, as in Wootton Fitzpaine.

Three flowers associated with ancient woodland include (*left*) narrow-leaved lungwort, found only in woods on clay soils in the south, (*right*) wood vetch, and (*opposite*) yellow archangel (seen here with wild garlic).

Place-names incorporating the word *hay* (a wooded hedge or woodland clearing) are also of interest. *Hay* is common throughout west Dorset, particularly in the Marshwood Vale (Childhay, Meerhay), and it is possible that the settlements in the Vale were carved out of dense woodland in medieval times in areas where the lias soils were too heavy to have attracted earlier settlers. Even today the farms and hamlets in the Vale are scattered, with their few villages on the peripheral drier land.

A very different approach to the search for ancient woodland involves using books, maps and documents in the archives of the Dorset Records Office and elsewhere. Documentary evidence has proved invaluable when there is doubt about an ancient woodland site. Historical studies and field observations can provide evidence for identifying ancient woodland. As we have seen already, there are references to woods and trees in Dorset from late Anglo-Saxon charters to Elizabethan surveys, and collectively these old historical records provide a valuable background.

Nine hundred-year-old Dorset Domesday records tell us which settlements at that time had woodland, and how much. Ancient woodland is unlikely to exist in places where none was recorded in 1086. Some woods are named in medieval documents and there can

be no doubt of their antiquity: Marley Wood near Winfrith Newburgh, West Wood at Coombe Keynes, Bagman's Copse near Woodlands, Wilkswood north of Langton Matravers, Burwood at Cranborne, and any number of Colewoods where charcoal was once made. There is also the evidence of some ninety medieval deer parks (see page 33) where deer turned woodland into wood pasture, and many court cases in which trees or underwood were stolen, or else destroyed by cattle.

By 1600 the art of map-making was established and so more precise information is available. Both county and estate maps become increasingly important in locating and identifying ancient woods. Woods in Blackmore, Cranborne Chase, Purbeck and Holt are shown on Tudor and early seventeenth century maps, and later, on maps made for landowners of some of the county estates. One example among many is an early estate map of Blandford in 1659 showing Broadley or Bradley Wood, mentioned in medieval records and now a plantation of conifers.

THE WORKING WOOD

Prior to the Industrial Revolution, Dorset's woods were its most important source of raw materials. There was hardly a skill or trade not reliant on timber. It could be found planked and stacked throughout the county, from the timber yard of the coastal shipwright to that of the humblest waggon builder. The mill wheels turning in the Stour or Piddle were built of wood. As charcoal, it heated the blacksmith's forge. Castles as well as cottages were dependent on timber; for roof trusses, rafters and floor boards. Dorset's woods provided fencing, tools, fuel for cooking, plough shares, bark for tanning – the list could lengthen indefinitely.

From the Middle Ages onwards there are records of manorial rights allowing pigs to forage through the woods in the autumn for beech-mast and acorns (*pannage*); or for *estovers*, the right to collect fallen wood for fuel, and *assarts*, by which woodland was cleared to provide

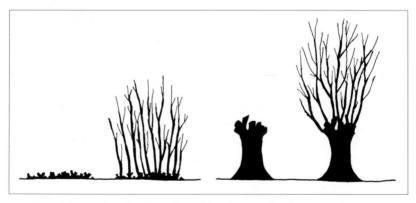

Coppicing and pollarding. Coppicing is woodland managed so as to produce underwood trees which are cut to ground level every few years and then grow again from the stool. Pollarded trees are cut about 10 feet above ground, and are more commonly found in mixed pasture and woodland where coppiced shoots would be at risk from deer or cattle.

grazing or arable. The court regulating the various rights in Gillingham Forest in Elizabethan times even refers to honey: 'if it bee in the Forest whoe hath it or of right ought to hath it.'

The varied structure of an ancient wood owes much to the skills of generations of woodlanders. The pits, banks, and ditches that help give old woodland its character survive as evidence of centuries of use. The familar stools of coppiced hazel hint at a whole range of traditional crafts; some of which were passed down from generation to generation.

Thomas Hardy's description of Giles Winterborne planting trees in *The Woodlanders* is a far cry from the way in which most are planted today: 'Winterborne's fingers were endowed with a gentle conjuror's touch in spreading the roots of each little tree, resulting in a sort of caress under which the delicate fibres all laid themselves out in their proper directions for growth. He put most of these roots towards the south-west; for, he said, in forty years' time, when some great gale is blowing from that quarter, the trees will require the strongest holdfast on that side to stand against it and not fall.'

COPPICING AND POLLARDING

Since earliest times woods have been managed to produce a continuous supply of timber and underwood. Timber or 'standard' trees were close-grown to promote development of tall, unbranched trunks which were felled at maturity. If trees were cut or coppiced when young, new shoots could be selected to grow into long and slender poles. Poles were easily handled and had dozens of uses in rural communities. Multi-stemmed trees are still a familiar sight in Dorset woods: oak, ash, alder, sweet chestnut, sycamore, and even small-leaved lime near Cranborne and in King's Wood, Purbeck. One of the ancient coppiced oaks in the Milborne Wood has a 19 feet girth and supports ten massive poles up to 2 feet across. Most coppiced oaks are smaller because they were regularly lopped to produce a renewable supply for firewood and charcoal-burning, and bark for tanning.

Hazel is commonplace in nearly every wood in the county and for centuries has been coppiced to yield rods and wands suitable for

Old hazel waiting to be coppiced in Garston Wood.

A hurdlemaker in a Dorset wood in the 1920s. The cleft hazel is woven between stout rods, set upright in slots in a wooden beam, which is then twisted round the end uprights so as to bind the hurdle together. An experienced hurdlemaker can make 10 hurdles in a day.

Coppiced oak in Milborne Woods, probably last coppiced over a century ago. The young shoots of a newly coppiced oak can grow up to 7 feet in a summer's growth. Oak was traditionally coppiced every 24 years or so, the bark providing tannin for leather, the timber everything from ladder rungs to wheel spokes,

making thatching spars, hurdles and other rural products. Where hazel is shaded, overgrown and uncut, it eventually fails to regenerate. The practice of coppicing has declined since the last century except in a few scattered woods, notably in Cranborne, Cranborne Chase and between Dorchester and Blandford. Now it is being revived in other woods and once overgrown hazel is being cut for firewood or charcoal-burning. New growth from cut stools is usually coppiced on a seven or eight year cycle, so that there are different stages of development within one wood as well as more light and space.

After coppicing, the increase in light encourages a profusion of flowers. Early purple orchids, dog violets, primroses and lesser celandine in Bere Wood, one of Dorset's ancient woods.

Pollarded trees, especially ash, were formerly cut about ten feet above ground to protect the regrowth from browsing cattle and deer, and old pollards are not uncommon on the boundaries of woods. Pollarded oaks of great age are a feature of ancient wood pasture, and can be seen in Holt Forest, at Badbury Rings and in Melbury Park.

Coppice-with-standards woodland can be managed in ways which benefit wildlife, yet still produce a profitable crop. Timber has to be extracted with minimal disturbance to other vegetation; old trees, fallen branches and stumps are left to rot; open areas are created; unwanted brash from coppicing is used to protect hazel stools from browsing by deer or to make dead hedges; unnecessary bonfires and tidying up are avoided; rides and paths are maintained, and some areas of woodland are left undisturbed. In contrast, unmanaged and neglected woods become increasingly shaded and lose the diversity of habitats essential for many woodland plants and animals. It takes much time and hard labour to revive them. A visit to a coppice-with-standard oakwood at bluebell time is one of the greatest pleasures of spring in Dorset.

ROYAL FORESTS & DEER PARKS

Dorset's Royal Forests, like those elsewhere in England, were created by the Norman kings from shadowy Saxon beginnings in the eleventh century. Their purpose was to provide hunting for the king and a habitat suitable for the beasts that came within the royal prerogative – wild boar, red, fallow and roe deer. Within their bounds 'the breeding, feeding and succouring of the king's deer' took precedence. In an age before refrigeration, deer were an important source of fresh meat, and hunting was both a sport and of practical importance. The Royal Forests also included the king's demesne woods, providing huge timbers for castles and abbeys.

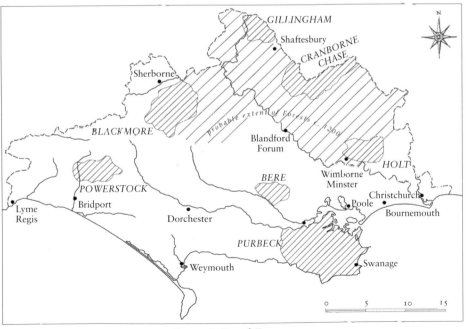

Dorset's Royal Forests.

Those living in Forests were subject to forest law. The vegetation on which the deer grazed and browsed (the vert) enjoyed the same protection as the deer themselves (the venison). Its laws were harsh and punishments severe. Poaching was punishable by death. The laws were upheld by a forester appointed by the king, who in turn employed lesser officials to bring offenders before the forest courts.

The unpopularity of forest law, and the pressure caused by a growing population hungry for land, led to their relaxation in the wake of Magna Carta (1215). A decline in woodland in Dorset's Royal Forests probably starts from this time, as woods once preserved by law gradually became pasture or arable land. By the seventeenth century none of the county's Royal Forests remained in the ownership of the crown. Most are now mainly farmland, and only Holt Forest continues to survive as a place-name on modern maps.

BERE FOREST

Bere Forest was possibly a forest prior to the Norman Conquest and appears to have been afforested by King John, who occasionally stayed in the manor. Later, the estate was granted to Simon de Montfort, though there is evidence that the wealthy abbey at Tarrant Crawford had claims on the Forest. Three centuries later, in 1546, Henry VIII granted the lordship of the manor of Bere to Robert Turberville, whose memorial brass is in Bere Regis church.

The Forest boundaries remain unclear, but must have extended south towards the heathlands near the River Piddle. Medieval records mention the 40 oaks assigned by the Sheriff of Dorset for building the manor house at Fordington. What is now Bere Wood has been replanted, but another medieval document may refer to various small woods nearby, which still have the rich flora characteristic of ancient woodland.

FOREST OF BLACKMORE

Much of what we now think of as the Blackmore Vale lay within the Royal Forest, including extensive estates held by the abbeys of Sherborne, Glastonbury and Cerne until their dissolution by Henry VIII. In the twelfth century the forest was enlarged to adjoin both Gillingham Forest and Cranborne Chase, incorporating settlements

A roe deer hind.

where there was woodland at the time of the Domesday Book.

The records relating to the forest provide typical examples of the uses its timber and brushwood were put to:

1227. . . in the wood of Middlemarsh, every weekday, one horseload of Alder, granted by the Abbott of Cerne to Master Henry of Cerne . . .

1233. . . sixty oaks to the Abbott of Bindon, for the fabric of his church.

1237. . . 20 tree stumps from the Forest of Blackmore to be carried to Tarent [Crawford] for fuel for the abbess . . .

. . . but at the end of the thirteenth century only small areas of woodland remained.

CRANBORNE CHASE

At approximately 250,000 acres Cranborne Chase was once the largest of Dorset's Royal Forests. It covered much of the north-east of the county, sprawling eastward into both Hampshire and Wiltshire. Its outer bounds extended from Shaftesbury to Salisbury, south to Ringwood, west to Wimborne and Blandford, then north to Shaftesbury. Later it was limited to inner bounds which included Ashmore, Farnham, Sixpenny Handley, Gussage St Andrew, Chettle, and Tarrant Gunville.

The Chase was divided into walks, whose woods were partitioned and named. From earliest time the ash and hazel on the chalk uplands were coppiced in rotation by hurdle-makers, who were allowed to enclose and protect their stands for up to seven years after cutting, after which leaps and creeps had to be made in the fences to allow deer to feed on the underwood and other vegetation. Fences were essential, because pigs and cattle were pastured in the woods at certain times of the year.

As elsewhere in the Royal Forests, the woods had to be productive. A record from the time of King John records Chase timber providing 100,000 shingle pins, nearly 14,000 shingles, and 1020 lengths of planking.

A few important Dorset woods are named in records of royal grants concerning the Chase, including Chetterwood, Oakley Wood, Burwood (near Cranborne), Blagdon Hill Wood, Castle Hill Wood (Edmonsham), High Wood (in Alderholt Park), and Garston Wood (near Sixpenny Handley), which is now one of the RSPB's most important woodland reserves. Significantly, the woodland flora is outstanding in those woods which are still broadleaved.

GILLINGHAM FOREST

Of all Dorset's Royal Forests, the records for Gillingham are the most extensive, though only isolated pockets remain wooded today. Gillingham itself was part of the royal manor of Dorchester and Fordington, and there are many references to the Forest to which it gave its name from the twelfth century until disafforestation by Charles I in 1625. At its greatest extent, the Forest adjoined Selwood Forest in Somerset, Blackmore south of the River Stour, and Cranborne Chase to the east.

An account of the privileges accorded one of its official foresters, or 'fosters', in 1474 provides a wonderful portrait of the way of life in the woods of medieval Dorset: 'The Foster shulde have going and pasturing in the Parke of Gillingham, winter and somer, 12 kine [cows] and a bull, 2 mares and their fooles, a sowe and her fare, and 16 oves [ewes] free, the left shulder of every seasonable dere tha kylled within the said park and forrest, all wyndfall wood that brekyth with the wynd, bringing upp no erthe in the rote of the tree.'

Nor were the other officials forgotten, for if the fallen tree brought up 'as moche erthe as will fill the flene [funnel] of a keepers horne' it then became the property of one of the rangers.

The 900-year-old Duncliffe Wood crowns the familiar rounded summit of Duncliffe Hill west of Shaftesbury. It is now owned by the Woodland Trust, who are clearing much of the conifer to help restore the canopy of native trees.

The Forest produced some fine timber, and thirteenth century records list an endless succession of purposes to which it was put, including (in 1315) 'repairs needed for Sherborne Castle from the time of the general Earthquake . . . '

By 1624, when the future Charles I leased the Forest to his former tutor, Sir James Fullerton, the former royal palace outside Gillingham had been abandoned and much of the Forest had been settled and cleared. A good example of this is near Motcombe, where settlements were carved piecemeal out of the woods, leaving a surviving mosaic of ancient hedges.

There is now no evidence of the great trees and woods of the medieval Forest. The only traces to survive are above Motcombe, at Cowridge, at Kingsettle, and near the Somerset border. Most of what once was forest is now lush dairy pasture. Happily, the woods on the southern slope of Duncliffe Hill, now owned by the Woodland Trust, were outside the Forest and escaped the wholesale felling that took place as soon as it was disafforested.

Holt Forest appears as the *Foresta de Wimburne* in the Domesday Book, and was originally part of the royal manor of Kingston Lacy, containing woods, wastes and heath, as well as settlements and cultivated land. The village of Holt, in the centre of the Forest, was granted the right to hold a fair and market, suggesting that some woodland had been cleared to provide open land for settlements. From Elizabethan times there are references to timber sales and the high cost of fencing. One document mentions the 990 'good oaks' in Duke's Copse (later renamed Queen's Copse). The oaks may have gone – 52 of them to 'the building of the Guild Hall in Blandford Forum' – but substantial sections of its boundaries can still be traced.

Holt ceased to be a Royal Forest in 1603, and was later acquired by Sir John Bankes when he bought Kingston Lacy. The modern Holt Forest (National Trust) is a place of oaks and holly on former wood pasture. Queen's Copse is now mostly conifer plantations, but here and there are traces of old coppices and the rare small-leaved lime of the medieval Forest woodlands.

POWERSTOCK FOREST

Powerstock was afforested some time after 1205 when King John acquired it in exchange for land in the manor of Fordington. A contemporary record refers to woods, now unknown, extending from Fordington Fields west of Dorchester north towards the Blackmore Vale.

The king made at least four visits to Powerstock, where the mound on which his castle once stood still survives. Few references to timber trees have been found, and the Royal Forest was probably already wood-pasture with enclosures and coppices managed by commoners when disafforested in the mid-fourteenth century. Today, what is now Powerstock Common includes a variety of plantations and regenerated woodland in the care of the Dorset Wildlife Trust.

FOREST OF PURBECK

The Isle of Purbeck is a good example of a Royal Forest that was largely heath and open waste, though the slopes of the Purbeck Hills are likely to have been more extensively wooded than they are today.

An ancient oak on Powerstock Common, and within the boundaries of the original Powerstock Forest.

In medieval times, red deer were plentiful, and in due course the Forest was designated a Warren so that its 'lesser beasts' – hare, rabbit, pheasant and fox – could also be hunted. Until Elizabethan times control of the Warren was vested in the Constable of Corfe Castle, a royal appointment backed by considerable powers.

The Constable was required to preserve the woods and control felling, though individual constables were not above breaking the laws they were supposed to enforce. In 1278, for example, the Abbess of Shaftesbury complained that the then constable 'has carried away 500 ashes, 2000 maples and thorns from her wood at Kingston, damaging 200 acres.' But good quality timber seems to have been scarce, and much of it was brought in, as at Corfe Castle in 1356 when '8 great oaks' from Holt Forest were used for 'making the bridge in the middle ward of the castle.'

DEER PARKS

At least ninety deer parks once existed in Dorset, and they were almost always in well-wooded land. Their heyday was between 1200 and 1500, and they can best be described as man-made outdoor larders. Their principal purpose was to supply fresh meat, specially during the winter, providing a more certain supply of venison than by relying on hunting. Deer confined in a park were cornered by hounds and trapped in nets. A few parks were large enough to be hunting grounds in their own right, like the 1000 acre Blagdon Park near Cranborne. Others held deer prior to their release for hunting, or as gifts to stock another park. Some belonged to the king, others to wealthy landowners, who could only 'empark' when granted a licence.

Medieval records generally refer only to 'deer', rarely distinguishing between red, fallow and roe. Until the early seventeenth century, red deer were plentiful on the heath around Wareham and on the heavier clays of the Stour Valley. Of the three, the roe is best suited to woodland, whilst the fallow preferred more open grazing, often where once dense woodland had thinned.

Deer parks usually occupied manorial waste that included woodland, rough pasture, scrub, and a stream. Most were fairly small, with a boundary a mile or two long. The earlier ones were enclosed by a massive bank set with stout oak pales, and with a ditch on the inner face. Later parks, such as Melcombe, Holt and Melbury Sampford, were not completely embanked, suggesting a shortage of timber. Harbin's and Holditch had 'deer leaps', cunningly built into the bank to allow free-roaming deer to jump in but not out.

Each park required enormous amounts of timber. The pales were up to 10 feet high, usually oak 'poles' coppiced on a 20 year cycle. A commission into Holt Forest in 1598 reckoned that over 8,000 trees were needed to maintain the 3½ mile long boundary of Holt Park for 30 to 40 years. Once the timber was exhausted, a thorn hedge replaced the palings, as at Gillingham Park, which by the sixteenth century was 'fenced with ditch and quickset.'

Trees and deer are not compatible. Young trees, saplings and the undergrowth from coppiced stools cannot endure constant fraying and browsing. Much of the woodland in the medieval parks must have failed to regenerate, leaving only a number of venerable lichen-covered oaks: as at Melbury, Badbury and East Lulworth. Most of the former deer parks are now agricultural land, and any ancient woods and coppices have only survived if protected by bank and ditch from grazing livestock; as at Clinger Park (Buckland Newton), or if they remained as woodland, as at Blagdon Park where a narrow strip still survives.

A detail from Robert Morden's map of Dorset of 1695. Two royal forests are named, Cranborne Chase and Holt, as are three deer parks (from north to south) Blagdon, Woodlands, Little Canford and Canford Magna.

The decline of the Dorset deer parks began following the Black Death in the fourteenth century, when labour was in short supply for making and repairing the pales. Severe winters and food shortages are also thought to have caused high mortality amongst the deer. By 1695, the date of Robert Morden's map of Dorset, the only parks shown are Athelhampton, Blagdon, Canford, Gillingham, Hooke, Marshwood, Melbury, Sherborne and Woodlands. Interestingly, of these, modern maps show only Melcombe and Woodlands, but also include Cerne and Harbin's Park (Tarrant Gunville). Modern parks that probably began life as deer parks are Canford, East Lulworth, Kingston Lacy, Melbury, and Sherborne.

RESTORATION & CONSERVATION

Viewing the heavily wooded landscape from the summit of Hambledon Hill you might think Dorset's woodlands need no conservation. Yet contained in that panorama are several nature reserves which demonstrate why woods need to be managed for wildlife. Many ancient woodlands were wholly or partly felled and replanted with conifers during the twentieth century. Now that their unique value is fully recognised, schemes to restore these 'planted' ancient woods by removal of non-native tree species are well under way. Time is pressing, as the survival capacity of dormant seeds of ancient woodland plants under conifers is limited. Obviously, the resurgence of characteristic species like bluebells, wood anemones and primroses is vital if the damaged woods are to retain their former glory. Care, however, has to be taken not to harm fragile soils nor to

To keep out deer in coppiced clearings in their Garston Wood Reserve on Cranborne Chase, the RSPB have built fences of woven hazel. By the time the fences rot, the coppiced hazel will be robust enough to survive occasional browsing.

A drift of lesser celandine and wood anenome in the Girdler's Coppice
Reserve managed by the Dorset Wildlife Trust, where regular coppicing has
helped improve the habitat for butterflies and other wildlife.

let in too much light too quickly so that brambles and bracken take
over. Deer damage is a constant problem.

A visit to Powerstock Common (DWT) or to the 900-year-old
Duncliffe Wood (WT), near Shaftesbury, will show the progress that is
being made to restore the canopy of native trees and bring back the
plant and animal life that once characterised Dorset's ancient
woodlands. Inevitably, such restoration projects are long-term.
However, year by year, through natural regeneration, some judicious
tree planting where necessary, widening of woodland rides and
creation of glades, and renewal of traditional coppice management,
the special atmosphere of these 'jewels in the woodland crown' can
once again be enjoyed.

Most of our small woods, as has been mentioned earlier, were run as coppice-with-standards. The periodic cutting of the hazel every 5 to 15 years created clearings, inspiring a profusion of spring and summer flowers in the first few years after coppicing, and in turn leading to a boom in birds, butterflies and other insects. To retain the community of plants and insects linked to coppicing the period of shade as the hazel regrows is equally important. Even now, some of the cyclical processes which determine our woodland wildlife are unclear, but retaining or restarting centuries old traditional methods of management is essential.

Before and after clearing rhododendron on Brownsea Island. Volunteer parties organized by the Dorset Wildlife Trust have helped grub out rhododendron, which since being introduced in the early nineteenth century has spread out of control in several parts of the county.

Butterflies are a useful indicator of the health of a wood.
Top left: The rare wood white has been reintroduced to one or two places
in west Dorset and might be seen in woodland rides in May and June.
Top right: The purple hairstreak is common in oak woods, where they fly
in July and August and on which the females lay their eggs.
Lower left: The tiny chequered black and white grizzled skipper flies
from April to June in woodland clearings, the female usually laying single
eggs on wild strawberry or bramble leaves.
Lower right: The increasingly rare white admiral is most likely to
be spotted around bramble blossom in July and August in open
rides and clearnings.

Bracketts Coppice near Corscombe is an excellent example of how research can help woodland reserve managers in the future. Its 28 hectares are diverse: pedunculate oak, ash, hazel and birch, with old pasture and a stream. Coppicing is carried out at the rate of 0.2 hectares of woodland per year on a 10 year cycle, which has opened up the heavily shaded woodland, with the result that coppiced clearings are now home to small pearl-bordered fritillaries, silver-washed fritillaries, white admirals and garden and wood warblers.

Butterflies are a useful indicator of the health of a wood: what is good for butterflies generally encourages other wildlife as well. The

Dorset Wildlife Trust leases two other woodlands near Sturminster Newton, Girdlers Coppice and part of Piddles Wood; whilst further to the east, near Sixpenny Handley, the RPSPB own Garston Wood. The wood is a superb example of ancient woodland on calcareous soil beneath the oak trees where hazels were cut every 10 years to supply poles for thatching spars and hurdles, and the RSPB continue coppicing it today. Thirty species of butterfly have been recorded and the regrowing coppice attracts nightingales and nesting turtle doves. The RSPB warden makes dead hedges of the cut poles around the coppice clearings to keep deer from browsing; a problem throughout Dorset, including the Woodland Trust's Duncliffe Wood, where conifers have been felled to reinstate deciduous woodland, only to find serious deer damage follows.

It must be said that woodland management is not just about felling trees – lichens and bryophytes on ancient trees depend upon their continuing long life. Veteran parkland trees occur at Lulworth Park and Kingston Lacy for example, and those in Melbury Park are pollarded to retain their traditional character. Ancient trees are particularly good for insects such as wood boring beetles, and standards in woodlands which are dead or contain a high proportion of dead wood are essential for wood wasps, tree creepers, owls and woodpeckers.

It would be unfair to ignore the contribution made by private landowners in looking after Dorset's wild places. Many farmers take great pride in their woodlands, hedges, grasslands and ponds, working closely with English Nature, the Farming and Wildlife Advisory Group, and DEFRA (Department for Environment, Food and Rural Affairs). There is no better example than one farm on the edge of the Blackmore Vale whose woods are coppiced, where thousands of trees have been planted, dormice are monitored, otters have been reintroduced on the river and the increase of breeding herons watched with great pride. Ultimately, the future of much of the countryside depends on the farming community.

Opposite: Old man's beard and guelder rose in autumn.

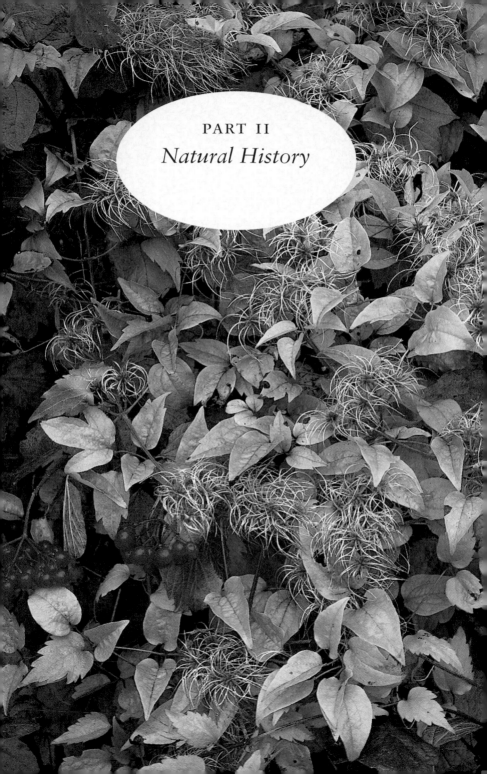

PART II
Natural History

DORSET WOODLAND

NATIVE WOODLAND TREES AND SHRUBS

The earliest records we have of Dorset trees are from Iron Age charcoal found at Maiden Castle near Dorchester, which included oak, ash, willow, poplar, birch, elm, whitebeam and yew. The smaller trees were represented by hazel, crab, common buckthorn, hawthorn, service-tree, plum, cherry and blackthorn. From other records we can add lime, field maple and holly.

Pedunculate oak, its acorns on stalks, dominates much of Dorset's broadleaved woodland. The sessile oak, more familiar in north and west Britain, is less abundant. Hybrids occur, also with the alien Turkey oak. The wildlife associated with woodland oaks is phenomenal because an oak tree can provide habitats for mammals, birds, moths, other invertebrates, insect galls, ferns, lichens, mosses, fungi, slugs and snails. Oak grows with holly and silver birch on more acidic soils, often with bracken or brambles. Silver birch rapidly colonises woodland clearings as well as damp heathland on sandy soils. Holly is heavily browsed by deer.

Ash grows alongside oak in many woods and is common on Dorset's chalk and limestone soils. Seedlings and saplings are plentiful but palatable and often eaten by deer. The ground flora is an expanse of dog's-mercury and ramsons, the pungent wild garlic. Old coppiced ash trees are a common feature of wood boundaries where branches, now massive, once were laid to form a hedge.

Field maple, which gives its name to Mapperton and Mappowder, grows with ash and hazel in many woods on the Dorset chalklands. It is also common in hedgerows; often with wayfaring-tree, common buckthorn, dogwood, spindle and hawthorn; sometimes with clematis and white bryony, and more rarely with whitebeam.

Sallow or grey willow is widespread in damp woods on poorly-

Oak and newly-coppiced hazel in Piddles Wood, near Sturminster Newton, one of the remaining oak woodlands in Dorset that dates back to the medieval period.

drained soils. Where it has taken over old ponds and abandoned wetland, a sallow wood or 'carr' develops. Marsh violets flourish in some sallow woods on west Dorset greensands, and in wet places the poisonous hemlock water-dropwort is well-established. Both the silver and downy birch trees are common in sallow carrs. Such woods are generally secondary woodland and develop rapidly when land drainage has been neglected.

Alder is a tree along water courses and springs and forms small areas of woodland in wet places. The trees are often multi-stemmed, evidence of past coppicing when alder was valued for its wood and charcoal. It is long-established in ancient woodland, hence such names as Aldermore and Alderholt.

Wych elm has survived the effects of elm disease in ancient woods, notably at Badbury. But the widespread loss of the elm has caused the decline of an elusive butterfly, the white-letter hairstreak. English elm is regenerating as suckers in many hedgerows, even spreading into woodland, as at Wyke Wood near Abbotsbury.

Small-leaved lime and wild service-tree, both uncommon in Dorset, are found only on sites of ancient woodland. Small-leaved lime grows in a dozen places, mostly in the north and east of the county, and only in long-established estate woodlands. Lime trees were once regularly coppiced and the trees at Edmondsham and on the Hampshire border are centuries old. Archaeological evidence shows that lime trees were abundant in Britain until the Bronze Age, but they have became increasingly rare because young trees, growing from suckers and occasionally seed, are palatable and constantly at risk from grazing animals. Small-leaved lime as a woodland tree appears to have been displaced gradually by the more prolific oak tree.

Wild service-tree is now restricted to a few woods and former woodland boundaries in Piddles Wood and elsewhere in the north and west of the county. Seedlings are rare, probably because the fruits are eaten by small mammals and birds, but established trees produce numerous suckers which can become trees if not coppiced, chewed by deer, or too severely shaded.

Crab apple is a rather uncommon and solitary tree in ancient woods. It is a small tree, once valued for its hard wood and as a rootstock for cuttings from other apple trees. Crab is distinguished by its dark and dense twiggy branches and small bitter fruits. Edible apples in woods are introductions near sites of habitation, often growing with elder bushes, nettles and other plants which need enriched soil.

Aspen is the only native poplar. It is locally frequent along the edges of damp woods on heavy soils, sometimes with the hybrid Grey poplars. Goat willow is a medium-sized woodland tree, and like sallow, an important food plant for caterpillars, and commonly occurs as a hybrid with other willows. Guelder rose may be found in the wetter woodland soils, and rowan, the mountain ash, in more acidic, sandy places. Gean or wild cherry was originally a native tree, but present trees are probably recent introductions.

Woodland hawthorn is almost unknown in Dorset but common hawthorn is in hedges everywhere, and on most wood boundaries where its fruits provide a bounty for birds in autumn. Blackthorn does not usually grow inside ancient woods, but soon invades clearings and spills out from wood edges on to pasture if not checked. Blackthorn scrub on old wooded commons or rough grassland is prominent at

Left: The wild service tree is one of Dorset's rarer trees. Its edible fruits are popular with birds and small mammals.
Right: An ancient ash tree. Old specimen trees are rare because of the popularity of its timber, which although lighter in weight than oak is as strong but more pliant: hence its traditional use for police truncheons!

Powerstock, Lydlinch, Deadmoor and Povington, and is an ideal habitat for nightingales in spring and butterflies in summer.

Yew in Dorset woods appears to have been planted or introduced by birds; the only yew wood, on the south slopes of Hambledon Hill, is believed to be medieval in origin. Whitebeam, too, has been widely planted on calcareous soils but native trees are also widespread, and may be seen in Garston Wood and other parts of Cranborne Chase.

HEDGES AND THICKETS

Hedges are crucial to wildlife. They are like linear woodland, extending along roads and fields, and linking woods and copses which have become isolated in farmland. Best in Dorset are ancient hedgebanks, the former boundaries of Saxon parishes, medieval deer parks, estate woodland, old tracks and drove roads. In these long-

Left: The remains of an ancient hedge on the Kingcombe Meadows Nature Reserve. The photograph on the right shows volunteers laying a hedge on the Reserve.

established hedges you may find dogwood, buckthorn, wayfaring-tree, spindle, hazel, holly, as well as honeysuckle, clematis, black bryony, white bryony, briars and brambles. Sometimes there is butcher's-broom, not uncommon in north-east Dorset, but this unusual shrub may have been planted to fill gaps. Old trees in a hedge are likely to have been pollarded, coppiced or laid, and the number of different trees and shrubs is often found to correlate with the antiquity of a hedgebank. The tangle of hedgebank vegetation provides many birds with excellent cover, nesting sites and a good supply of food. More than eighty kinds of moth caterpillars feed on hawthorn leaves alone. Hedgebanks are habitats where fox, badger and rabbit dig their holes. The deep, shady sides of hollow-ways, where a lane is lower than the fields each side, is ideal for ferns, mosses and liverworts. Less shady places may have primroses, violets and other woodland plants. A few hedges are the sites of Dorset rarities: wild tulip, small teasel and copse-bindweed.

Recent hedges have less diversity than old ones. Hedges along the rectangular fields of farmland were planted with elm, hawthorn or holly and other shrubs when the open landscape was enclosed during the eighteenth century and later. Few mature elms have survived the devastating beetle-carried fungus responsible for Dutch Elm disease, but elm suckers are again a familiar feature. Newer hedges are lacking

Wild flowers at the foot of a Dorset hedge, including bluebells, wild garlic, campion and yellow archangel.

in woodland wild flowers but they are important sites for nesting and feeding birds, as well as corridors for bats and barn owls. When overgrown hedges are cut back by mechanical flailing and slashing, the shrubs eventually recover, but birds are forced to establish new territories. The revival of the art of hedge-laying in the Blackmore Vale, at Lower Kingcombe and other parts of Dorset has shown that a stockproof hedge may be a profitable alternative to a wire fence.

Most thorn thickets and scrub have been cleared from Dorset farmland; juniper is virtually extinct though thorn, gorse and brambles continue to invade ungrazed chalkland. Thorn and sallow thickets develop wherever there are abandoned pastures on soggy soils, including the unstable coastal undercliffs. All kinds of thickets are valuable bird habitats and left undisturbed become colonised by ash, maple and oak and eventually develop into natural woodland.

Other changing habitats are important. Of special interest are Dorset's young oak plantations on several estates, especially in the Blackmore Vale, as well as many roadside and other plantings of broad-leaved trees throughout the county. They are wildlife sites of the future and their natural history is unfolding.

Many woods are a mixture of broad-leaved trees and conifers, and include both introduced and native species. Where they were planted or became established on old pasture or arable land they have no resemblance to ancient woodland, but those planted on sites of former woodland still have hazel with bluebells, sedges and woodrush and other woodland flowers.

Beech trees are common in Dorset woods, and are a familiar sight around parkland and estates, along boundaries and as avenues near Kingston Lacy and on Cranborne Chase. Many have originated from plantings beginning in the second half of the eighteenth century. Few shrubs and flowers can grow in the heavy shade cast by beech apart from a few rare orchids and fungi. The tree does not appear to be a native in Dorset, and has been widely introduced as a timber tree in modern plantations such as the Gardiner Woods above Springhead. It is often grown with conifers which act as 'nurses' to help the saplings become established.

Beech in mixed woods may be associated with other introductions: sycamore, sweet chestnut, horse chestnut, Turkey oak, common lime,

Beech and other broadleaved trees in Hooke Park in autumn.

Like other small mammals, the common shrew is resident in mixed woodland. As its surface area is large in proportion to its weight, much energy is expended in the time-consuming search for food: beetles, earthworms, snails and other invertebrates.

and poplars in damp spots. Holm oak is a useful evergreen. Mature hornbeam is rare. Conifers include European and Japanese larch, Scots and other pines, red cedar, Norway spruce, Douglas fir, and Western hemlock. They are generally grown for timber in blocks but single trees are common in estate woodland, often with Wellingtonia and coast redwood.

When some of the older estate woods were established to provide cover for game birds, alien shrubs such as snowberry, *Lonicera nitida*, laurel, box, and the invasive *Rhododendron ponticum* were introduced. Now many estate woods are overgrown and heavily shaded. Where there is ground flora, the difference from ancient woodland is obvious because the flowers of ancient woods are absent. In their place are nettles, ivy, hogweed, goosegrass, rough meadow-grass, herb robert, Yorkshire-fog, brambles and elder bushes. Sometimes a wood has signs of settlement or ridge-and-furrow from former farmland. Most estate woods have walls or fences and lack the conspicuous hedgebank-and-ditch of ancient woods.

The wildlife of these mixed woodlands is generally less plentiful and varied than in ancient woodland, but there are commonly habitats for pheasant, deer, grey squirrels and probably most of the woodland mammals. Bird life depends on available shelter and sources of food.

Insects and other invertebrates occupy suitable places. Fungi appear in the autumn and the commoner lichens slowly become established on tree trunks.

CONIFER WOODLANDS

Scots pine was introduced into eighteenth century estate woodlands and the heathland of south-east Dorset where pine readily regenerates. Long established pines on the islands of Poole Harbour and around Bournemouth are distinctive landscape features, contrasting sharply with the formal plantations on twentieth century estates where conifers of various kinds have been planted as timber trees. Notable conifer plantations, sometimes with lesser stands of broad-leaved woodland, are at Champernhayes, Chetterwood, Cranborne, Farnham, Duncliffe, Holt Forest, Hooke, Lulworth, Melbury, Middlemarsh, and Blandford. Other extensive plantations on former heathland are those of the Wareham, Puddletown and Ferndown Forests, now managed by Forest Enterprise, and include plants of heath and heath bogs in open areas.

Plant and animal life is sparse among conifers compared to broadleaved woodland, and much poorer than in the countries from where the trees originated. Blocks of trees in a plantation tend to be of one species, age and size and usually cast heavy shade. There may be birdlife and plenty of insects but vegetation tends to be restricted to mosses, ferns and fungi able to tolerate low levels of light. In several ways, conifers can influence the soil: their needles are slow to rot, leaf litter becomes increasingly acidic and buried seeds may not survive.

The picture changes when there are additional habitats in conifer plantations: grassy rides; damp spots with sallow, birch, rowan, holly and Molinia grass; patches of bracken, bramble or heather; or old trees, stumps and fallen branches. Rides and clearings can be good places to find foxglove, fleabane and flowers of acidic grassland, also perhaps bilberry bushes or climbing corydalis, and, near Moreton, the rare heath lobelia. Areas where wood sorrel, wood spurge, woodrush and bluebells struggle to survive among the trees clearly indicate that the place was once ancient woodland.

Many insects are well adapted to living among conifers: longhorn

Left: A spotted longhorn beetle, found in pine woods from June to early August.
Right: A wood ant pulling a leaf towards its colony's nest of twigs, leaves and grass stems.

beetles in stumps, bark beetles on pines, several pine-shoot moths and pine weevils in young shoots, numerous micro-moths and other moths on bark, including the pine hawk-moth, and the caterpillars of the bordered white moth on needles. The well-known wood-ant builds spectacular nests, constructed by thousands of worker ants from fallen needles, especially pine and spruce, and associated with the 7-spot ladybird. Three of Dorset's thirty-four ladybird species live on conifers, and two heathland butterflies, the grayling and silver-spotted blue occur in heathy places among pine trees. Flying insects provide food for bats, but bat boxes need to be provided if permanent bat colonies are to be established. Both bat and bird-nesting boxes are being set up in Forest Enterprise plantations.

Dorset conifer forests have encouraged the rapid spread of sika and roe deer as the ranks of trees provide ideal cover when deer extend their territory. Roe bucks and Sika stags cause a lot of damage by fraying bark when they rub velvet from their antlers. Foxes, grey squirrels, and short-tailed voles are other common animals in many conifer plantations, and small populations of red squirrels survive among the mature pines of Brownsea and other Poole Harbour islands.

PLANTS

FLOWERING PLANTS AND FERNS

Woodland flowers are at their best in spring before the trees come into leaf and when there is more light and less competition from shrubs. Dorset's ancient coppiced woodland is especially rich in wild flowers. Many are found in the deep and slightly acidic loams of bluebell woods, some in drier chalk soils among dog's-mercury and wild garlic and others in woodland of all kinds.

As mentioned in Part I, some plants grow only in ancient woods and coppices and are not found in secondary woodland: herb-paris, toothwort and yellow gagea; pale sedge and thin-spiked sedge; the three woodrushes, greater, hairy and southern woodrush; and the grasses, wood melick and wood millet. Ferns in woodland include hard fern, hard shield fern, scaly male fern and polypody, but most ferns can also grow in damp, shady hedgebanks where there are other familiar woodland flowers: primrose, violets, goldilocks and Dorset's 'spring messenger', the lesser celandine. Other plants, normally confined to ancient woodland and unable to spread to new places

Wild garlic (ramsons) in old woodland near Milton Abbas.

Left: Goldilocks is the only woodland buttercup.
Right: Wild daffodils beneath hazel near Edmonsham.

include wood anemone, yellow archangel, bitter-vetch, wood vetch, wood spurge and the rare narrow-leaved lungwort of south-east Dorset. Wood anemone has proved to be an especially reliable indication of a site of ancient woodland wherever it grows.

Several familiar plants grow in both old woods and old pastures: wild daffodil, locally common on heavy soils in a narrow band across the county from the Devon border east to Edmondsham; meadow saffron, restricted to a few places such as Horse Close Wood in central Dorset, and pignut and betony, widespread on more acidic soils. Plants of old pastures such as lady's-mantle, long-stalked crane's-bill and adder's-tongue fern are to be found in the grassy rides of several ancient woods. Rides are also places where butterflies may feed on plants such as bugle, wild strawberry and common fleabane.

Woodland orchids grow in the humus-rich soils of both ancient woods and more recent plantations, notably beech. The helleborines seem to favour wood margins, especially on chalkland soils. Others, including bird's-nest orchid, tolerate deep shade, and some, including early-purple, butterfly and fly orchids, also grow in grassland. Orchid capsules full of minute seeds may be seen on old flower spikes at the end of the summer, but deer are a serious threat in some Dorset woods

Three of Dorset's rarer flowers are (*left*) toothwort,
(*centre*) bird's nest orchid and (*right*) violet helleborine.

because they nip off the flowering spikes before the capsules can form. It is probable that insect pollinators are present in woodland, although self pollination is common in white helleborine and other orchids.

Wet places in woods are habitats for other plants. Damp spots often have clumps of wild red currant, possibly spread by birds; small streams are commonly lined with golden-saxifrage, including the rarer opposite-leaved golden-saxifrage in west Dorset; in a few wet woods there is water avens and its woodland hybrid. As well as ferns, sedges are usually plentiful, and more rarely, wood clubrush and wood horsetail, also in the west of the county.

Only a few plants can tolerate heavy shade in summer and the two saprophytes, yellow bird's-nest and bird's-nest orchid, are rare and hard to find. Other summer flowers are commoner in clearings and glades: hairy St John's-wort, orpine in Piddles Wood and a few other places, nettleleaved bellflower on the Purbeck Hills and other chalk slopes, yellow pimpernel on clay, common cow-wheat and golden-rod on more acidic soils.

Some of Dorset's rarest plants are found in a single or else only a handful of places. Spring snowflake grows in a stream-side coppice in west Dorset, solomon's-seal in a wood in Cranborne Chase, and plants once used for medicine or poison, monkshood, mezereon, green hellebore and stinking hellebore, occur in places which suggest that long ago they may have been introduced. Certainly, lily-of-the-valley and snowdrops in Dorset woods are recent introductions, but columbine was probably a wild plant before being brought into cottage gardens. Whatever their origin, these attractive plants add to the variety of Dorset's woodland flowers.

LICHENS, MOSSES AND LIVERWORTS

All woods have a selection of lichens, mosses and liverworts, familiar groups of plants not always easy to identify. Only a few have common names. Many are epiphytes, and grow on tree trunks and branches. Others grow on the ground, especially at the base of trees. They depend on the damp atmosphere and moist soil typical of woodland. Dorset has good places for lichens; many of the 500 British lichens of shrubs and trees can be found in the county, except those formerly associated with mature elm trees, now dead. There are suitable sites in parks and damp, open woodlands where conditions are favourable: sufficient light, air relatively free of sulphur and other pollutants, little disturbance and a continuity of old trees. Oakers Wood near Bovington has an exceptional number of different kinds of lichens. Recent studies of these small plants have been encouraged by their role as indicators of clean air. They do not harm trees and may hide insects and provide useful nest material for long-tailed tits and other songbirds.

The main groups of bark lichens – leprose, crustose, foliose, and fruticose – are well represented. The nature of the bark is important, its texture, acidity and position on the tree. Many kinds of lichen can be found on hazel and holly, and on the rougher bark of ash, maple and oak. The venerable oak trees in the wood pasture of Melbury deer park are renowned for many rare species, including *Lobaria amplissima*, one of the four lungwort lichens.

[55]

Left: The lichen *Cladonia fimbriata* is common on woodland stumps and tree bases, principally in woodland on acid soils.
Right: The edible parasol fungi is found in clearings and open rides.

Mosses often share a 'mini-habitat' with lichens, liverworts and even green algae. They grow tightly in tufts, clumps, patches or cushions wherever conditions are suitable for them to get established. Mosses such as *Dicranum majus, Frullania tamarisci, Plagiothecium undulatum,* and *Rhytidiadelphus loreus* are found in ancient woodland. Wet and shady woods are ideal for *Plagiorinum undulatum* and *Thamnobryum alopecurum,* and liverworts such as *Lophocolea cuspidata* and *Plagiochila asplenioides.* Common woodland mosses include species of *Atrichum, Eurhynchium, Hypnum, Mnium, Orthotrichum, Ulota,* pale cushions of *Leucobryum glaucum* and the beautiful, fern-like *Thuidium tamariscum.*

FUNGI

Fungi in woods are mostly unseen, their fungal threads or hyphae feeding on leaf litter, twigs, droppings and fallen branches, helping to create humus and enriching the soil with nutrients. They are an indispensible part of the cycle of decay and renewal in woodland life, and promote tree growth when their hyphae are united as mycorrhiza with tree roots.

The appearance of larger fungi, better known as mushrooms or toadstools, is irregular and unpredictable. These fungal fruiting bodies are capable of producing astronomical numbers of reproductive spores. A toadstool may be restricted to one type of woodland: on poor, acid soils under conifers or birch, or richer soils under oak, or chalky soils under beech. Some grow only in unusual habitats: a pine cone, an oak leaf, a dead insect, a pile of dung, an old bonfire site. Most species occur countrywide and are not confined to any one county. Dorset woods provide good habitats and fungi are plentiful in ancient woodland: for example, Bracketts Coppice in north Dorset has over 400 species.

Conspicuous fungi have been given English names: parasites such as dryad's saddle, on ash and several other trees, slimy beech caps on old beech trees, beefsteak fungus on oak, honey fungus on many trees; saprophytes such as sulphur tuft and orange pholiota on stumps; stinkhorn under conifers; milkcaps and bright-coloured russulas under mature trees; brain fungus and witches butter on branches. A special group are the symbiotic fungi in lichens on bark and stumps.

A collection of fungi found on a Dorset Wildlife Trust 'fungus foray' in the autumn. Fungi are plentiful in Dorset's woods: Bracketts Coppice near Halstock has over 400 species.

Edible fungi are also well-represented in Dorset woods and include wood mushroom, wood blewitt, cep or penny bun, and hedgehog fungus in mixed woods; chanterelle, usually under oak, horn-of-plenty in deep moss; oyster mushroom on fallen branches; cauliflower fungus at the base of mature conifers; and in most woods, more russulas and milkcaps. A wood with clearings or grassy rides may have other edible species: parasols, shaggy inkcap, even giant puffball.

Fungi poisonous to man are widespread: the deadly death-cap and other *Amanita* in many woods, fly agaric under birch, and several brown-spored species of *Hebeloma, Entoloma, Conocybe* and *Inocybe* – all of which are best left untasted. Yet mushrooms and toadstools are regularly eaten by deer, badgers, squirrels, voles, woodmice, snails, slugs and the larvae of numerous beetles, flies, gnats and micro-moths. Fungi may be an important source of food for many creatures before winter sets in, and there is a strong case against over-collecting in autumn.

Amongst Dorset's invertebrates are the cardinal beetle and the stag beetle, both of whose larvae live under the bark of rotten tree stumps.
Left: The cardinal is found in June along hedgerows and wood margins, whilst the unmistakable male stag (*right*) is the giant among British beetles, the largest reaching three inches in length.

ANIMALS AND BIRDS

INVERTEBRATES

Insects live in all kinds of Dorset woodland and make use of every available habitat. Over 200 different insects have been found on oak trees alone and in ancient woods there may be several thousand, some uncommon and others familiar, in both larval and adult form.

Ground beetles and springtails are plentiful in soil and leaf litter, and flies and dung beetles wherever there are animal droppings. Other beetles include cardinal beetles, stag beetles and longhorns which occupy rotten tree-stumps, together with earwigs, sawflies and hover-flies. Other creatures at ground level are centipedes, millipedes and woodlice, slugs on fungi and succulent plants, spiders, mites and ticks, including the disease-carrying deer tick. Earthworms occur in soil which is neither too wet nor too acidic. Snails of several kinds are plentiful in lime-rich woodland soils and may be preyed upon by glow-worm larvae, whilst the presence of others may indicate if the soil had ever been grassland.

Large numbers of insects live on tree trunks, including the ash bark beetle and the notorious elm bark beetle, responsible for spreading the fungus which destroys elm trees. Other examples from Dorset woods are the larvae of moths such as the red-necked footman which feed on lichens, and robber flies, snake flies and bark bugs which feed upon insect larvae. Many moths and micromoths are concealed on bark by their cryptic colouring. Bumble bees, hornets and tree wasps make nests in tree holes, and honey bees colonise convenient hollows.

The leaves of most woodland trees are liable to attack from insect larvae, especially in spring. The green oak tortrix caterpillars can defoliate oak trees, and both buff-tip and winter moth caterpillars damage various broadleaved trees. Other leaf insects include species of bugs, weevils and other beetles, as well as leaf miners.

The silver-washed fritillary is the largest and most magnificent of
the British fritillaries and is found in older woodland
between June and September.

Large numbers of insects and other invertebrates are eaten by birds
and small mammals. Whilst shrews and hedgehogs are concealed
among leaf litter and fallen branches, birds are active at all levels in
well-structured woodland. Crane-flies, gnats and mosquitoes are
taken by flycatchers, whilst once night has fallen other flying insects,
including cockchafers and dung beetles, are eaten by woodland bats.

Thirty-eight of Dorset's butterflies breed in woods. Each has special
requirements and depends on woodland structure, wood margins and
the land beyond. Other essentials are oak or other trees, shrubs,
brambles and climbers, a continuity of coppicing, sunny glades,
flowers in spring, winding paths, open grassy rides and damp, flower-
filled ditches. Woodlands in such places as Cranborne Chase,
Deadmoor, Powerstock and Bracketts Coppice are rich butterfly sites
because they provide many of these features.

The purple emperor is rarely seen in Dorset. Even more elusive is
the white-letter hairstreak, which requires mature elm. In the larger
oakwoods there are colonies of both purple hairstreak and white
admiral, and, depending on coppicing and the availability of common
dog-violet, the fritillary butterflies, pearl-bordered, small pearl-
bordered and silver-washed. The high brown fritillary is apparently
restricted to a single Dorset wood.

The white-letter hairstreak was once plentiful in Dorset's woods and hedgerows in July and August, but the loss of the elm to Dutch Elm Disease has robbed it of what was its principal food plant.

Some butterflies such as hedge and meadow browns, marbled and other whites, dingy and grizzled skippers, are common in woodland glades and grassy rides. In shadier places and among shrubs are holly blue, speckled wood, green hairstreak and brimstone, the latter attracted to common buckthorn on chalkland and purging buckthorn on acidic heathland soils. Many colonies of woodland butterflies disappeared during years when hazel coppices were abandoned and became overgrown and shady. With the renewal of coppicing in both private woods and nature reserves, butterflies have a better chance of survival, and the re-introduction of a few species, notably the wood white in west Dorset has proved a success.

REPTILES AND AMPHIBIANS

Different habitats in woodland may be occupied by other animals such as reptiles. Woodland clearings, especially when stumps and branches have been left, are warmer and lighter than in surrounding woodland and suitable for adders and grass snakes. Toads are not uncommon, and there are likely to be frogs and newts feeding on aquatic insects in ponds. All the British snakes and lizards of heathland may also inhabit sandy clearings in mature pine plantations.

A great spotted woodpecker feeding a fledgeling.

BIRDS

Birds of woodland in lowland Britain are well represented in Dorset. Garston Wood in Cranborne Chase is a good example of old woodland where birds are plentiful. Here there are trees and shrubs of all ages and a wide range of habitats: perches, song posts, tree stumps, nesting sites and a supply of food. The ground layer of the wood provides a constant food supply: small plants, mosses, seeds, acorns, insects, spiders worms, snails, as well as leaf litter and dead branches to hide in. Then the 'field' layer with its ferns, flowering plants, low bushes and brambles, is ideal for scrub warblers and other small birds. The higher undergrowth of thorn trees, coppiced hazel or other shrubs provides nesting sites for thrushes and blackbirds. Above, in the tree canopy, willow warbler, wood warbler and chiffchaff feed among the leaves, and on branches near the tree-tops, woodpigeons, crows, buzzards and sparrowhawks can make their nests.

Holes and hollows in standing trees are ideal nesting sites for the nuthatch, tree creeper, great spotted woodpecker and tawny owl. Glades and more open areas are hunting-grounds for the spotted

The tawny owl usually nests in a tree hole, laying between 2 and 4 eggs, and is the most common of Dorset's owls.

Above: A green woodpecker feeding its young.
Opposite page: A winter visitor from northern Europe, a redwing on holly.

flycatcher. Young hazel coppice is suitable for nesting garden warblers. Thickets inside the wood attract nightingales in spring, and brambles provide winter shelter for redwing, fieldfare, redpoll, even brambling, as well as resident birds. Woodland territories are established by most of the familiar birds of gardens and hedges: robin, blackbird, wren, dunnock, song thrush, mistle thrush, bullfinch, greenfinch, and all the common tits.

The fortunes of woodland birds in recent years have been mixed. Some, like the blue tit and the green and spotted woodpeckers have fared well while the populations of birds such as willow and marsh tits, thrushes and lesser spotted woodpeckers have declined. The causes are not fully understood and new research has been launched.

A few birds are attracted to pine plantations in search of insects and nest sites. The green woodpecker digs into wood ant nests, and the great spotted woodpecker feeds on bark insects and conifer seeds. Goldfinch, chaffinch and various tits are often among younger trees, and siskin and goldcrest are not uncommon in tree-tops. Jays, magpies and wood pigeons are generally frequent and dead trees are important perches for birds of prey, including the hobby. Birch trees and sallow on the edge of plantations are additional habitats for tits and summer warblers. In winter, the crossbill occasionally arrives from the north to feed on the seeds of pine cones.

Some estate woodland, originally planted with beech, chestnut or sycamore, often has a dense undergrowth of rhododendron and other alien shrubs with little birdlife. Where pheasants are reared, finches

and other seed-eaters take advantage of their food, whilst damp, grassy rides may attract woodcock. However, as has been emphasised earlier, Dorset's planted woods lack the diversity of habitats found in long established broadleaved woodland.

MAMMALS

Deer are the largest woodland mammals and have a profound effect on their habitat. They damage trees by fraying the bark, prevent natural regeneration by eating tree seedlings and saplings, and retard the regrowth of coppiced hazel.Where young trees are protected by tree-guards and fencing, unprotected areas become more vulnerable. Large herds of deer eventually destroy undergrowth and turn well-structured woodland into wood pasture, or 'high forest', with only mature trees. Dorset woods are home to roe, fallow, sika and muntjac deer. The few red deer are rarely seen, and are the descendants of those that once escaped from parks. Muntjac, a recent arrival in Dorset, are small and secretive creatures, but are becoming more widespread. Sika were introduced to Brownsea Island in the last century and escaped to the mainland. Herds of sika are not uncommon in and around the conifer plantations of the heathlands of south-east Dorset and are extending their range.

Fallow deer are long-established in the county and are still kept in a few parks, notably Stock Gaylard, but most now browse in well-wooded places such as Powerstock and Cranborne Chase, where they do considerable damage in hazel coppices as well as on the surrounding farmland.

Roe deer are widespread wherever there is woodland. In ones or twos they emerge to feed at dawn and dusk, ranging over farmland, hedges and gardens before hiding in dense thickets during the day. They are bigger than the roe of eastern England and their numbers are on the increase. Unlike other deer they fray tree-bark in spring, when trees are most vulnerable. They feed on a wide range of plants, including grasses and herbs, tree shoots, leaves and berries. In winter, deer activity can be assessed by the degree of browsing on holly shoots before the new shoots of coppiced hazel and ash are attacked in spring.

Top: Sika deer in their summer coats. Sika were originally introduced to Brownsea Island in Victorian times, but following their escape are now becoming widespread, whilst the tiny muntjac (*bottom*), no larger than a labrador and introduced from China in 1900, is a recent arrival whose numbers are growing, particlarly on Cranborne Chase.

Fourteen species of bats occur in Britain and all have been recorded in Dorset. They are nocturnal and may be seen flying at dawn and dusk when they feed almost exclusively on insects. Many places are important for their food supply, ponds, marshy meadows, old pastures, hedges and trees. Although their natural roosts are woods and caves, most bats also use buildings for their summer roosts, and underground crevices in which to hibernate.

They also make use of hollows in trees and stumps, thickets and scrub, old hedgebanks with tall pollards, and continuous hedges linking summer roosts to feeding areas. Insects are plentiful in conifer

The bank vole is happiest in deciduous woodland, scrub, banks and hedgerows where there is plenty of cover.

plantations but natural roosting places are lacking. The long-eared bat is not uncommon in mature woodland. Only the serotine and greater and lesser horseshoe bats do not use hollow trees, but like other species they take advantage of woodland borders for spring feeding.

The two very rare species, Bechstein's and Leisler's, may depend wholly on mature woodland. The noctule, barbastelle, pipistrelle, Daubenton's, whiskered and probably Brandt's bats may choose either trees or buildings for their summer roosts and trees for hibernation.

Many other mammals spend at least part of their time in woodland, even water vole, otter and mink where river banks are adjacent. Hedgehogs inhabit open woodland as well as hedges. Both the common shrew and pygmy shrew live in woods where there are hollows, stumps, grasses and rushes, and plenty of insects to eat. The bank vole and short-tailed or field vole can also survive in grassy parts of woods, particularly where tree guards provide 'safe houses' in young plantations. They eat almost anything and in turn are food for larger animals and birds of prey. Two closely-related mice, the elusive yellow-necked field mouse and the long-tailed field mouse inhabit woods, and the latter, confusedly called a wood mouse, is also common in gardens and hedgebanks. All these small animals may be active both day and night throughout the year. Only the hedgehog and dormouse are true hibernators.

The smaller mammals tend to be shy and retiring, so it is difficult to

One enemy of the bank vole is the weasel, whose diet also
includes shrew, mice, squirrels, moles, nesting birds and their eggs.

be certain of their numbers and spread. Apart from sightings other
records depend on live trapping-and-release, or from victims of cats or
pieces of bone in owl pellets. There may also be indirect signs such as
teeth-marks on nuts, tracks in mud or a small stockpile of flowerbuds.
The dormouse, protected and rarely seen, attracts more widespread
interest. It is known to live in several Dorset woods where coppiced
hazel is dense enough for its arboreal habits. Dormice need plenty of
nuts, which is encouraged by a longer coppice rotation, and re-
introduction programmes are going on in several Dorset reserves.
Blackerries and the haws of hawthorn provide alternative food, and
strands of old honeysuckle may be used in their nests, together with
moss, twigs, leaves and grass. Summer nests are high up in the bushes,
and winter nests are among brambles or on the ground, in and under
cut hazel stools. Dormice also make their nests in nest boxes designed
for birds.

Signs of other animals are common: badger setts, rabbit burrows,
fox earths, mole hills, even the 'form' of hares, a reminder that woods
give shelter in an insecure countryside, particularly in winter. Foxes,
weasels and stoats are well-known predators but polecats and pine
martens became extinct in Dorset by the middle of the last century.
Grey squirrels, the well-established 'tree rats' from North America, are
widespread and numerous. They destroy birds' eggs and cause
extensive damage to most trees, attacking bark, fruits and shoots. They
have displaced red squirrels in woodland throughout England. In

Dorset, red squirrels survive in small numbers among the pine trees of three Poole Harbour islands, including Brownsea. Great efforts are being made to save the red squirrel and dormouse from extinction in Dorset by protecting their habitats and managing woodlands to meet their particular requirements.

Circumstances often change our preconceived ideas about conservation. A history of neglect, deer damage and the uncontrolled spread of rhododendron are familiar problems to the National Trust and the Dorset Wildlife Trust on Brownsea island, where an unusual form of conservation woodland management is employed. Most naturalists have little time for Scots pines, primarily because they encroach on heathlands and support less wildlife than deciduous trees. Those on Brownsea Island are essential for the survival of Dorset's remaining red squirrel population, which feeds on the cones. The pine woodlands are surprisingly rich on the Island, supporting nesting herons, woodcock and nightjar, as well as bats and many insects.

After the 1990 storm, when many Scots pines were blown down, the Trust embarked on a system of clearance and fencing off deer and rabbit free areas. Scots pines growing in open conditions produce most cones, so woodland is thinned to provide room for young trees to grow. The work has been much-praised, and in 1996 the Dorset Wildlife Trust was awarded the Forestry Authority's 'Centre of Excellence' award for red squirrel conservation and public access on Brownsea.

Brookland Wood, near Fontmell Magna – one of three 'community' woods in Dorset recently planted to mark the millennium.

WOODLANDS FOR THE FUTURE

The extremes of woodland loss suffered nationally during the twentieth century did not occur on quite so dramatic a scale in Dorset. Many of the county's largest woods are in the hands of private landowners, whose estates often bear witness to a long history of careful stewardship. One only has to think of Melbury, Edmonsham, Milton Abbas, Crichel, Wimborne St Giles or Lulworth to be reminded of the debt owed to past and present generation of owners and their foresters. The same is true of the farming community, custodians of the innumerable small woods and copses that patchwork the county. Here there is already a tentative revival of the past economic role of woodland thanks to various enterprises being set up to harvest woodland produce – for furniture, fuel, charcoal, restoration work and garden features.

Dorset is fortunate in having many woodlands in the care of conservation bodies, notably the Dorset Wildlife Trust, the Woodland Trust, National Trust, and RSPB, well-supported by local authorities and their countryside services.

An encouraging recent idea is that of planting entirely new woods of between 10 and 25 acres near to villages for the benefit of future generations. Go to Brookland Wood (Fontmell Magna), Vecklands (Yetminster), or Hazel Wood (Hazelbury Bryan) and see the new community woods of the future. Created under the umbrella of the Woodland Trust for the 'Woods on your Doorstep' millennium lottery project, they are designed and looked after by the local community.

It is good to think that Dorset's woods, old and new, again have people, paid or unpaid, working within them and finding refreshment from the pressures of modern life. Like our forebears, we can enrich the environment our grandchildren will inherit, while enjoying the fine woodland legacy they left to us.

VISITING WOODLAND

Not every wood in Dorset can be visited but a wide variety are cared for by conservation bodies, local authorities and the Forestry Commission who all welcome walkers provided that care is taken not to disturb wildlife. In many woods access is only along public footpaths and bridleways, so it is essential to have the relevant O.S. maps with you and to follow path signs.

KEY: DCC: Dorset County Council, DWT: Dorset Wildlife Trust, EDDC: East Dorset District Council, EN: English Nature, FC: Forestry Commission, NNR: National Nature Reserve, NT: National Trust, PBC: Poole Borough Council, RSPB: Royal Society for the Protection of Birds, WT: Woodland Trust.

ALLINGTON HILL, BRIDPORT (SY 457935) [WT]. 42 acres of mixed woodland and open land on prominent hill to the west of Bridport. New plantings aim to extend the present woodland cover.

ARNE NATURE RESERVE, NR. WAREHAM (SY 984985) [RSPB]. Renowned for its extensive heathland and marshes, this large nature reserve includes both broadleaved – and often wet-woodland (eg Arne Big Wood) and coniferous forest. RSPB car park at reserve entrance near Arne village. Displays, guided walks, events.

ASHLEY WOOD NATURE RESERVE, NR. BLANDFORD (ST 928048) [DWT]. 30 acres of ancient hazel and ash coppice woodland with oak standards. Coppice management being revived. On north side of busy B3082. Parking very limited.

BENINGFIELDS WOOD, NR. BRIDPORT (SY 504972) [WT]. 20 acres of new broadleaved woodland in valley nr. West Milton planted in memory of Gordon Beningfield, the wildlife artist.

BLOXWORTH AND BERE WOOD, NR. BERE REGIS (SY 870950) [PRIVATE]. Ancient woodlands, partly replanted with conifers, between Bere Regis and Bloxworth, north of the A35. Access restricted to single bridgeway. Limited parking in Bloxworth village.

BRACKETTS COPPICE NATURE RESERVE, NR. HALSTOCK (ST 514074) [DWT]. 114 acres of varied broadleaved woodland and neutral pasture. Much of the wood is managed as coppice. Outstanding site for butterflies. Includes Birch Common, formerly wood pasture, but planted with conifers which will be removed over time.

BROWNSEA ISLAND, NR. POOLE (SZ 025882) [NT-DWT]. Wooded island in Poole Harbour with both broadleaved and pinewoods. Famous for surviving red squirrels, and tree-top heronry. 250 acre DWT nature reserve included much wet woodland and sallow carr. Visitor Centre, guided walks, leaflets. Boats from Poole Quay and Sandbanks.

BUGDENS COPSE LOCAL NATURE RESERVE, VERWOOD (SU 088088) [EDDC]. Ancient woodland in the heart of Verwood. Oak-hazel coppice birchwood and grassland. Traditional management being revived.

DELCOMBE WOODS, MILTON ABBAS (ST 785059-806036) [PRIVATE & FO]. Fine beech woods. Road from Woolland Hill car park to Milton Abbas takes you through them. Fine display of bluebells.

DELPH WOODS, POOLE [PBC]. Urban woodland by Broadstone.

DUNCLIFE WOOD, NR. SHAFTESBURY (ST 826222) [WT]. Over 200 acres of woodland set on prominent hill near Shatesbury. Ancient woodland being returned to its original condition after large parts were replanted with conifers.

FIFEHEAD WOOD, FIFEHEAD MAGDALEN (ST 773215) [WT]. 50 acres of ancient oak-ash woodland, part coppiced. Fine bluebell and butterfly site. Wet underfoot in places.

GARSTON WOOD NATURE RESERVE, NR. SIXPENNY HANDLEY (SU 004194) [RSPB]. Traditionally managed coppice woodland on Cranborne Chase. Some areas being left to mature as high forest. Good for butterflies and birds such as nightingale, turtle dove, spotted flycatcher and garden warbler. Small car park.

GIRDLERS COPPICE – See Piddles Wood.

GREENHILL DOWN NATURE RESERVE, NR. HILTON (ST 792037) [DWT]. 30 acres mainly downland but includes coppice woodland. Access via public footpath from Hilton, above Milton Abbas.

HAMBLEDON HILL YEW WOOD, NR. BLANDFORD (ST 850114) [EN (NNR]. Part of large downland NNR. Access to wood by permit only, but good views from road below near Hanford.

HATCHARDS COPSE, WEST MOORS (SU 076034) [EDDC]. Small block of ancient woodland off Station Road, West Moors. Revival of traditional coppice management. Also wet meadow and grassland. Small car park.

HAZEL WOOD, HAZELBURY BRYAN (ST 747093) [WT]. A good example of a newly planted broadleaved woodland of the future by the WT Woods on your Doorstep scheme. Others are Brookland Wood (Fontmell Magna), Little Giant Wood (Stoke Abbott) and Vecklands (Yetminster).

HOLT WOOD AND FOREST, NR. VERWOOD (SU 030060 & 038055) [NT/EN] (NNR). Two ancient wood pastures included in a mainly heathland NNR. Mostly oak with some beech and understorey of holly, birch and sallow. Magnificent spreading oak trees formerly pollarded.

HOLWAY WOODS, NR. SHERBORNE (ST 633200) [DWT]. 40 acres of mixed deciduous woodland and rough grassland. Foot access by permissive footpath.

KINGCOMBE MEADOWS, NR. TOLLER PORCORUM (SY 545985) [DWT]. Amid this 421 acres of ancient farmland with superb hedgerows, mature trees and scrub are small copses such as Red Holm Coppice with a canopy of birch, oak and alder.

KINGSETTLE WOOD, NR. SHAFTESBURY (ST 865002) [WT]. 51 acres of woodland in prominent position just north of Shaftesbury. Being returned to broadleaved woodland after part planting with conifers.

KING'S WOOD, PURBECK (SZ 000816) [NT]. Beechwood on north slope of Purbeck Hills. Access from B3351.

KINGSTON LACY WOODS, NR. WIMBORNE (ST 970030) [NT]. The coppiced High Wood and The Oaks, both by Badbury Rings, are two of the woods of interest on the NT's Kingston Lacy Estate. Short walk from Badbury Rings car park. Also a woodland walk round the edge of Kingston Lacy Park is attractive passing some impressive beech areas. From the Pamphill car park it is a short distance to Abbott's Copse 986007 where the spring bluebell display is spectacular.

LAMBERT'S CASTLE HILL, NR. MARSHWOOD (SY 370986) [NT]. Hilltop with a belt of wild woodland on the north escarpment.

LANGTON WEST WOOD, NR. LANGTON MATRAVERS, SWANAGE (SY 991795) [NT]. Part of the NT Corfe Castle Estate which covers large areas of Purbeck. The wood is part of the ancient belt of deciduous woodland on the north-facing slope of the valley to the west of Swanage.

LEWESDON HILL, NR. BEAMINSTER (ST 437013) [NT]. 27 acres of mixed ancient woodland, dominated in part by massive beech, clothing the highest hill in Dorset. Approachable by public footpaths eg. from Broadwindsor but parking very limited.

METLANDS WOOD, NR. FRAMPTON (SY 625945) [DCC]. Mixed woodland just south of the A356 in Frampton. Walkers car park nearby at Tibbs Hollow. Firm paths suitable for wheelchairs.

MOORS VALLEY FOREST, NR RINGWOOD (SU 106047) [FC/EDDC]. Adjoins country park with all visitor facilities. Good example of modern productive forest with coniferous plantations, forest walks, tree-top trail, and measures to improve the forest environment for wildlife and people.

OAKERS WOOD, NR. MORETON (SY 810915) [PRIVATE]. Fine deciduous wood accessible on foot only along the bridleway running N-S. Parking at FC Culpeppers Dish park.

PENNINGTONS COPSE, WEST MOORS (SU 092095) [EDDC]. 17 acres on the western edge of West Moors village. Oak standards with hazel coppice. Rhododendron being cleared. Includes an Alder bed. Coppicing of Hazel and Alder part of current management. Footpath from village centre.

PIDDLES WOOD AND GIRDLERS COPPICE, NR. STURMINSTER NEWTON (ST 797127) [PRIVATE (HINTON ST. MARY ESTATES) PART DWT LEASE]. Large ancient woodland in the Blackmore Vale traditionally managed as hazel coppice with oak standards. Part planted with mixed conifer and broadleaf trees. Coppicing of Hazel restored. DWT Nature Trail and other rights-of-way through wood. Small car park near Broad Oak for nature trail. Use Fiddleford Mill car park for Girdlers Coppice.

POWERSTOCK COMMON, NR. TOLLER PORCORUM (SY 540973) [DWT]. 285 acres of ancient oak-ash-hazel woodland with coppice, hedgebanks and heathy grassland NW of Eggardon Hill. Parts of the former common replanted with conifers are gradually being returned to native broadleaved trees. Exceptional site for butterflies and a rich flora and fauna. Small car park at SY 547974. Network of rides for walkers.

PUDDLETOWN FOREST, NR. DORCHESTER (SY 740930) [FC]. Large coniferous plantations south of the A35 east of Dorchester. Access from Rhododendron Mile road south of Puddletown. Forest walk.

STONEHILL DOWN NATURE RESERVE, NR. CORFE CASTLE (SY 925823) [DWT]. Situated on the Purbeck hills, the Reserve includes woodland on the north-facing slope above East Creech. Very limited parking near reserve entrance at foot of Creech Barrow.

STUDLAND WOODS, NR. SWANAGE (SZ 035835) [KNOLL CAR PARK NT] [NT (NNR)]. Studland Heath NNR includes wet woodland (Pipley Wood) at end of Little Sea lake near car park. Woodland Trail through the woodland. Also Studland Wood by Old Harry Rocks on coastal footpath from Studland is of interest.

THORNCOMBE WOOD, NR. DORCHESTER (SY 726922) [DCC]. Mixed woodland near Hardy's Cottage at Higher Bockhampton. Woodland trail. Car Park.

TROUBLEFIELD NATURE RESERVE, NR. HURN (SZ 125978) [DWT]. 15 acres of mainly wet grassland by Moors River but including damp deciduous woodland important for birds.

TWO-MILE COPPICE, NR. WEYMOUTH (SY 674821) [WT]. 14 acres, partly ancient woodland, close to Weymouth.

TURNWORTH WOOD, NR. OKEFORD FITZPAINE (ST 810085) [NT]. 134 acres of old deciduous woodland and grassland. Foot access from Okeford Hill car park (DCC) via ridgeway.

WAREHAM FOREST, NR. WAREHAM (SY 905895) [FC]. Large coniferous forest north of Wareham. Access from car parks on Wareham-Bere Regis and Sandford-Morden (B3075) roads (eg. Sherford Bridge.) Wareham Forest Way walk traverses the forest. Extensive views of the forest from Woolsbarrow (SY 893926).

FURTHER READING

Allaby, M., *The Woodland Trust Book of British Woodlands*, 1986
Bettey, J.H., *The Landscape of Wessex*, 1980
Cantor, L.M. & Wilson, J.E., *The Medieval Deer-Parks of Dorset* (Dorset Procs., Vols 83-100), 1961-1978
Colebourn, P. & Gibbons, R., *Britain's Countryside Heritage*, 1990
Edlin, H.L., *Trees, Woods and Man* (The New Naturalist, 32), 1956
Hawkins, D., *Cranborne Chase*, 1980
Hoskins, W.G., *The Makng of the English Landscape*, 1955: with additions by C. Taylor, 1988
Marren, P., *Britain's Ancient Woodland*: Woodland Heritage, 1990
Rackham, O., *Trees & Woodland in the British Landscape*, 1990
   The History of the Countryside, 1986
Wake Smart, T.W., *A Chronicle of Cranborne and The Cranborne Chase*, 1841

ACKNOWLEDGEMENTS

I would like to thank woodland owners who have been generous with their permission to visit their woods, and for the opportunities to meet Dorset hurdle-makers and other woodlanders. My appreciation is also extended to the staff of the Dorset County Museum, the Institute of Terrestrial Ecology, English Nature, the Dorset Environmental Record Centre and the Dorset County Record Office for their patient help.

I am grateful to Bill Copland for researching and writing 'Visiting Woodlands' and the following for allowing the use of so wonderful a selection of illustrations: Tony Bates; pages 10, 26, 31, 33, 38 (both), 39, (lower right), 46 (right), 54 (left, centre), 56 (both), 57, 70: Dorset County Museum; 24 (bottom); Bob Gibbons; front cover, 4, 9, 11, 15, 19, 20 (both), 21, 24 (top), 25, 36, 37, 39 (top right), 41, 45 (both), 46 (left), 47, 51 (both), 52, 53 (both), 54 (right), 58 (both), 60, 61: Royal Commission for Historical Monuments (England); 13: Colin Varndell; back cover, frontispiece, 29, 39 (top left, bottom left), 43, 48, 49, 62, 63, 64, 65, 67 (both), 68, 69.

INDEX

The
DISCOVER DORSET
Series of Books include

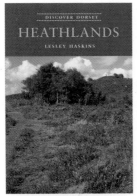

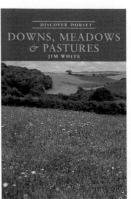

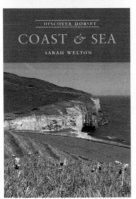

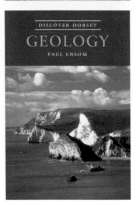

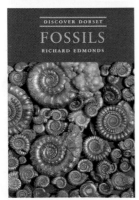

All the books about Dorset published by
The Dovecote Press
are available in bookshops throughout the
county, or in case of difficulty direct from the
publishers.
The Dovecote Press Ltd, Stanbridge,
Wimborne, Dorset BH21 4JD
Tel: 01258 840549
www.dovecotepress.com